Totally Tropical Rainforests

Calling all aliens!
Are you planning a holiday to planet Earth?
Finn and Zeek are here to help.

'Totally Tropical Rainforests'
Published by MAVERICK ARTS PUBLISHING LTD

Suite 1, Hillreed House, 54 Queen Street,
Horsham, RH13 5AD, +44 (0)1403 256941
© Maverick Arts Publishing Limited September 2024

A CIP catalogue record for this book is available at the British Library.

ISBN 978-1-83511-015-7

Printed in India

www.maverickbooks.co.uk

Credits:
Finn & Zeek illustrations by Jake McDonald, Bright Illustration Agency
Cover: Jake McDonald/Bright, © GUDKOV ANDREY/Shutterstock
Inside: © Sara Winter/Shutterstock (6), © Teo Tarras/Shutterstock (8-9), © FootageLab/Shutterstock (11), © Robin Lardon/Shutterstock (12), © SL-Photography/Shutterstock (13), © PixieMe/Shutterstock (14), © Alessandro Pierpaoli/Shutterstock (14), © usernameadam1/Shutterstock (15), © mbarredo/Shutterstock (15), © Kylie Nicholson/Shutterstock (16), © VOJTa Herout/Shutterstock (16-17), © Mark Green/Shutterstock (18), © Mark_Kostich/Shutterstock (18), © COULANGES/Shutterstock (18), © Dirk Ercken/Shutterstock (19), © Ondrej Prosicky/Shutterstock (19), © Enrico Pescantini/Shutterstock (19), © fernandoalonsostockfilms/Shutterstock (20-21), © PARALAXIS/Shutterstock (22-23), © Sergey Uryadnikov/Shutterstock (24), © Marco Lissoni/Shutterstock (25), © Enrico Pescantini/Shutterstock (27)

This book is rated as: Gold Band (Guided Reading)

Totally Tropical Rainforests

Contents

Introduction	6
Lots of Layers	10
From the Top	10
To the Bottom	12
Pretty Plants	14
Cool Creatures	16
People in Rainforests	20
Deforestation	22
Impact	22
Conservation	24
Quiz	28
Index/Glossary	30

INCOMING MESSAGE

Dear Finn and Zeek,

We're about to visit Earth and have heard about its amazing tropical rainforests. What should we know about them before we go?

From,
Leef and Drip
(Planet Sloff)

Introduction

It's in the name: rainforests are forests where it rains a lot!

There are two types of rainforest: temperate and tropical.

Temperate rainforests are found in cooler places than tropical rainforests. Countries where temperate rainforests are found include Canada, Chile, New Zealand, Japan and the USA.

Temperate rainforest in Canada

We're going to look at tropical rainforests!

Tropical rainforests are found in the tropics (the warm regions of the Earth running around its middle).

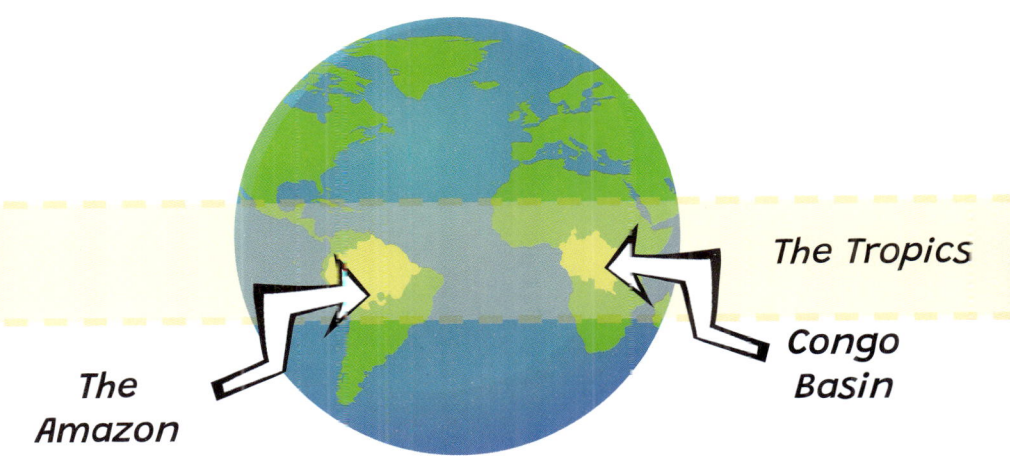

The largest tropical rainforest in the world is the Amazon. The second largest rainforest is found in the Congo Basin in Central Africa. This is big, but still much smaller than the Amazon rainforest!

Tropical rainforests can get at least 200cm of rain in a year. That's a lot!

With all this rain, you'd think that the soil in the rainforest would be perfect for plants. But actually, it rains so much that **nutrients** can be washed out of the soil, making it harder for plants to grow.

Remember your waterproofs when you're visiting the rainforest!

Tropical rainforests have no seasons. The temperature stays roughly the same throughout the year. Tropical rainforests are warm — mostly between 20 and 30°C! They are also humid, which means that there is a lot of water vapour in the air. These warm and damp conditions are great for plant growth!

Tropical rainforest in Costa Rica

Lots of Layers   From the Top

Tropical rainforests can be split into layers:

- The emergent layer
- The canopy layer
- The understorey
- The forest floor

The **emergent layer** is where the tallest trees are. They can be as tall as 14 double-decker buses. Some trees in the emergent layer can be around 1000 years old!

The **canopy layer** is thick with trees and plants. These limit how much sunlight can reach the ground below. Rain is also slowed down by the canopy, sometimes taking minutes to reach the rainforest floor. This layer is where you can find the most animals!

Lots of Layers To the Bottom

If you're in a Central or South American rainforest, the understorey layer is where you might find sloths climbing around!

There is lots of shade down in the **understorey layer**. It is very warm and humid. Shorter plants, shrubs and bushes grow in this layer.

The bottom layer is the **forest floor**. It's so dark down here that plants find it hard to grow. The ground is covered with **decaying** leaves which have fallen from trees and plants above. Insects and **fungi** help to break down the leaves.

Rainforest floor

Pretty Plants

Rainforests contain over half of the Earth's animal and plant species! This huge variety of plants and animals means rainforests are very important for preserving **biodiversity**.

There are lots of strange and beautiful plants in the rainforest.

These cocoa tree pods contain cocoa beans, used to make chocolate!

Lianas are woody vines. They wrap themselves around other plants and climb trees to try and reach sunlight.

Passion fruits grow in the rainforest. They are sweet and juicy!

Plants in the rainforest have adapted to their environment in clever ways:

- Lots of rainforest plants have smooth leaves with pointy ends so rain can run off them easily without causing damage.
- Mosses and **lichens** have adapted to survive with very little light.
- Epiphytes (like the one below) are plants which get nutrients from water and the air rather than soil. This allows them to grow on trees high up in the canopy layer.

Cool Creatures

Plants and trees in the rainforest provide humans with lots of useful things, such as coffee, fruit, spices, oils and plants which can be used to make medicines.

Rainforests also provide homes and food for many animals!

Check out this stunning Blue Morpho butterfly!

The rainforest is full of amazing creatures. Bats, birds and butterflies fly around tall trees in the emergent and canopy layers. Sloths and howler monkeys can be found hanging around the trees in Central and South American rainforests, while the rainforests of Central Africa are home to gorillas.

Jaguars (like this one) and black panthers might be spotted prowling on the forest floor!

Green anaconda snakes live in South America's rainforests. They can be almost 10m long and can swim!

Pink river dolphins swim into flooded areas of the Amazon rainforest.

Lots of animals have adapted to life in the rainforest in interesting ways:

Poison dart frogs are brightly coloured to warn predators that they are poisonous.

Some hummingbirds have very long and thin beaks to feed from tube-shaped flowers.

Sloths are so slow that green algae can grow on their fur, acting as **camouflage** amongst the plants!

People in Rainforests

Around the world, many different **indigenous communities** live in tropical rainforests and have been doing so for thousands of years.

Around 6000 Yagua people live in the Amazon rainforest in Peru and Colombia. The Yagua people have their own language and hunt rainforest animals including sloths and monkeys.

Yagua children in the Amazon rainforest

Some indigenous communities are 'uncontacted'. This means that they have little to no contact with the world outside of their community.

Deforestation Impact

Rainforests are under threat from deforestation. This is when trees are cut down for wood or to clear space for human activities like crop farming, animal grazing and mining.

About 20% of the Amazon rainforest has already been lost to deforestation!

Deforestation can have many negative impacts:

- Trees store **carbon dioxide**. Fewer trees means that more **greenhouse gases** are in the air, adding to **global warming**.
- Indigenous communities are forced to leave their homes.
- Animal habitats are destroyed. This can lead to some species becoming endangered or even extinct.

Deforestation   Conservation

Indigenous communities play an important role in conservation efforts.

Rainforest conservation means protecting rainforest areas from being damaged by humans. It is important to protect tropical rainforests and the people and animals that live in them.

Ways to Help the Rainforest

- Ecotourism can help protect rainforests. This is a type of tourism that focuses on protecting the local environment.
- Trees can be replanted in deforested areas.
- Governments and companies can make promises to protect certain areas of rainforest from deforestation.
- People can protest against deforestation.

MESSAGE SENT

Dear Leef and Drip,

Tropical rainforests are beautiful places that are home to many people, animals and plants. It is very important that humans protect them!

We hope you have fun and manage to spot a sloth in the trees!

From,
Finn and Zeek :)

Look at this sloth!

Quiz

1. Which is not a type of rainforest?

a) Temperate

b) Tropical

c) Leafy

2. Where is the largest tropical rainforest in the world?

a) The Amazon

b) Malaysia

c) The Congo Basin

3. How many layers are in a tropical rainforest?

a) 1

b) 3

c) 4

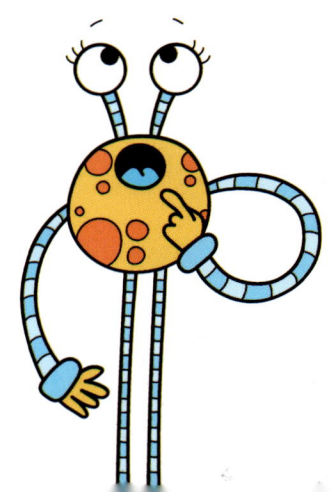

4. Which is the bottom layer of the tropical rainforest?

a) The understorey
b) The forest floor
c) The canopy layer

5. What is used to make chocolate?

a) Lianas
b) Fungi
c) Cocoa beans

6. What is deforestation?

a) When areas of forest are protected
b) When trees are cut down
c) A type of tourism

Index/Glossary

Biodiversity pg 14

A large number of different plants and animals living in the same place.

Camouflage pg 19

When something's appearance blends into its surroundings.

Carbon Dioxide pg 23

A greenhouse gas which is absorbed by trees and plants and released when they are burned.

Decaying pg 13

When something is breaking down and rotting.

Fungi pg 13

A type of living thing that grows on decaying or living plants.

Quiz Answers:

1. c, 2. a, 3. c, 4. b, 5. c, 6. b

Global Warming pg 23
The warming of the Earth's climate due to a build-up of greenhouse gases in the atmosphere.

Greenhouse Gases pg 23
Gases which trap heat in the Earth's atmosphere.

Indigenous Communities pg 20, 21, 23, 24
Communities of people who have lived in certain areas for many generations and are descended from the people originally living in those areas.

Lichens pg 15
A living thing that grows on surfaces like trees and walls.

Nutrients pg 8, 15
Substances which help living things to grow and be healthy.

Book Bands for Guided Reading

The Institute of Education book banding system is a scale of colours that reflects the various levels of reading difficulty. The bands are assigned by taking into account the content, the language style, the layout and phonics. Word, phrase and sentence level work is also taken into consideration.

Maverick Early Readers are a bright, attractive range of books covering the pink to white bands. All of these books have been book banded for guided reading to the industry standard and edited by a leading educational consultant.

Fiction

Non-fiction

To view the whole Maverick Readers scheme, visit our website at www.maverickearlyreaders.com

Or scan the QR code above to view our scheme instantly!